# On the Wild Frontier

## by Betty Verovitz
### illustrated by Laurel Aiello

ISBN 0-15-317228-2 – On The Wild Frontier

Ordering Options
ISBN 0-15-318615-1 (Package of 5)
ISBN 0-15-316986-9 (Grade 2 Package)

2 3 4 5 6 7 8 9 10  179  02 01 00

A long time ago, families traveled to the frontier. It was a hard trip across wild land. But one by one, they made up their minds to go. They wanted to tame some land and make new homes in the West.

Families had to plan their trips to the frontier. They needed horses, cows, and hens to start their new lives on the frontier. They needed wagons in which to carry their food and clothes and tools. They needed oxen to pull their wagons.

What did people take to eat? They
took a lot of different foods. They
needed dried fruits and vegetables.
They took flour, rice, eggs, tea, and
salt. They took some dried meat, too.
They also hunted for meat along
the way.

Families began their trips in the spring.
That was the nicest time of year. It was safer
for them to travel west in groups. People
helped each other survive dangers. What do
you think some of the dangers were?

People needed to be careful of the wild
animals, which were sometimes nearby.
The land was hard to travel on. There
were muddy rivers for the wagons to float
across. There were mountains to climb.
Also, the weather could be too cold or
too dry.

There were other things to fear on the
way, too. The storms could be very strong.
Some people got very sick, and others were
bitten by snakes. There wasn't always food
to eat. The people could get very hungry.

Families also had fun on the trail.
Children played tag and other games. The
boys and girls liked to play with their pets,
which they had brought from home. At
night, families sang together by the fire.

Children had chores to do along
the way. They found fruit, fresh water
to drink, and wood for the fire.
Children also helped bake bread and
watch for danger.

Families stopped in different places.
Sometimes when one family stopped to
make a home, other families found land
nearby. Then these families could help each
other. People stopped before winter because
it was hard to survive on the trail in winter.

Families had to build their homes
before the snow came. They needed
shelter from the weather. Most people
used wood to build their houses. They
helped each other to make the work
go faster.

When spring came, people cleared
the land. Then they could plant
vegetable gardens and apple orchards.
They used seeds from home. The
gardens and orchards grew on the
frontier lands.

Why did families travel to the frontier?
They wanted to make new homes. They
wanted to tame the land and to farm.
They wanted to plant orchards.

What are some new frontiers today?
Why might families want to travel there?

# Frontier Facts

Read each sentence below. Then number a sheet of paper from 1 to 10. Write *T* if the sentence is true. Write *F* if it is false. (Turn the page to find the answers.)

1. Families did not take meat on the trip.
2. The children played tag and other games.
3. There was no way to bake bread on the trip.
4. Families took dried fruits and vegetables on the trip.
5. Families left on their trips in the winter.
6. Wagons sometimes had to be floated across rivers.
7. The trail was flat all the way across the country.
8. People did not take pets on the trip.
9. Before winter, people built houses.
10. In spring, families cleared the land.

TAKE-HOME BOOK
***Something New***
Use with "Johnny Appleseed."